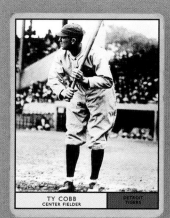

TY COBB
CENTER FIELDER

DETROIT
TIGERS

HANK GREENBERG
FIRST BASEMAN

DETROIT
TIGERS

THE STORY OF THE DETROIT TIGERS

Published by Creative Education
P.O. Box 227, Mankato, Minnesota 56002
Creative Education is an imprint of The Creative Company
www.thecreativecompany.us

Design and production by Blue Design
Art direction by Rita Marshall
Printed by Corporate Graphics in the United States of America

Photographs by Getty Images (Walter Bibikow, Lisa Blumenfeld, Mark Cunningham/MLB Photos, Focus on Sport, Stephen Green/MLB Photos, Dave Kaup, Bruce Kluckhohn, MLB Photos, Ronald C. Modra/Sports Imagery, National Baseball Hall of Fame Library/MLB Photos, Pictorial Parade, Rich Pilling/MLB Photos, Tony Ranze/AFP, Mark Rucker/Transcendental Graphics, Herb Scharfman/Sports Imagery, Ezra Shaw, Ron Vesely/MLB Photos)

Library of Congress Cataloging-in-Publication Data

LeBoutillier, Nate.
The story of the Detroit Tigers / by Nate LeBoutillier.
p. cm. — (Baseball: the great American game)
Includes index.
Summary: The history of the Detroit Tigers professional baseball team from its inaugural 1901 season to today, spotlighting the team's greatest players and most memorable moments.
ISBN 978-1-60818-040-0
1. Detroit Tigers (Baseball team)—History—Juvenile literature. I. Title. II. Series.

GV875.D6L43 2011
796.357'640977434—dc22   2010024397

CPSIA: 110310 PO1381

First Edition
9 8 7 6 5 4 3 2 1

Page 3: Right fielder Sam Crawford
Page 4: Pitcher Jeremy Bonderman

BASEBALL: THE GREAT AMERICAN GAME

THE STORY OF THE DETROIT TIGERS

Nate LeBoutillier

CONTENTS

CLAWING INTO EXISTENCE

Named after the French word for "strait," Detroit, Michigan, is just that—a city on a river connecting two larger bodies of water. Settled in 1701 on the Detroit River between Lake Huron and Lake Erie by French officer Antoine de la Mothe Cadillac, Detroit grew to a population of 1,000 by the late 1700s. During pre-Civil War times, Detroit was an important hub in the underground railroad network that transported southern slaves to freedom in the North. From the late 1800s onward, Detroit rose in population due to its location as a gateway to the expanding West and to the automobile boom of the 20th century.

Detroit jumped into major league baseball in 1881 with a National League (NL) team called the Wolverines. That club lasted only eight seasons, as the city—then still relatively small—struggled to draw and retain talented players. But in 1901, three years before the new Ford Motor Company would really put Detroit on the map, a new club from

Detroit has earned several nicknames, including "The Motor City," for its automobile manufacturing, and "Motown," for its rhythm and blues music.

PITCHER · JACK MORRIS

Although Jack Morris never won the Cy Young Award, he was one of the most reliable pitchers of his time. In his 18-year career, he tallied 10 or more wins in 14 seasons—and 3 times totaled 20 or more. He started the Tigers' 1984 world championship campaign off right by hurling a no-hitter on April 7, the first of his 19 wins that season. Morris's fiery pitches were matched by his fierce nature; he often found himself in feuds with reporters or spats with teammates. Still, his strong arm was missed when he left the Tigers to play for the Minnesota Twins in 1991.

JACK MORRIS
PITCHER

DETROIT
TIGERS

STATS

Tigers seasons: 1977–90

Height: 6-foot-3

Weight: 200

- **5-time All-Star**

- **254 career wins**

- **2,478 career strikeouts**

- **1991 World Series MVP**

"The Motor City" began playing in the new American League (AL). Due to the black-and-yellow striped socks that were part of the players' uniforms, the team was named the Tigers.

The Detroit baseball team that began play in 1901 quickly lived up to its namesake's reputation for ferocity. In the club's first game, played on April 25, 1901, at Detroit's Bennett Park, the Tigers trailed 13–4 before staging a roaring comeback that left them with a 14–13 victory. The team finished a respectable 74–61 in that first season behind such players as outfielder Jimmy Barrett and shortstop Kid Elberfeld.

The Tigers suffered losing seasons after that until 1905, when they finished 79–74. That year, the Tigers featured a rookie by the name of Ty Cobb. A scrappy, nail-spitting outfielder who hailed from Georgia, Cobb batted just .240 in 150 at bats that season. It would be the only season in his 24-year playing career that he didn't top the .300 mark. The brash young player was as notoriously mean as he was talented. "Ty Cobb is a lowdown, miserable excuse for a human being," said outfielder Sam Crawford, another early Tigers star. "He's also the best player I've ever seen."

Cobb hit .350 to win the AL batting title in 1907, and the rest of the Tigers began to shine, too. The club's leading pitcher was "Wabash" George Mullin, a flamethrowing workhorse with control problems who was as likely to lead the league in complete games as walks, wild pitches, or hit batsmen. The Tigers of 1907 won the AL pennant with a 92–58 record before losing to the Chicago Cubs in the World Series. The next two seasons, the Tigers returned to the World Series but suffered two more defeats, first to the Cubs and then to the Pittsburgh Pirates.

The Tigers assembled some up-and-down seasons after that, but in Cobb's playing career, the Tigers would never again see the World Series. The 1915 season was particularly frustrating. Cobb hit .369 with 99 runs batted in (RBI) and 96 stolen bases as the Tigers finished with 100 wins and just 54 losses, but the Boston Red Sox finished with 101 wins, then easily won the World Series over the Philadelphia Phillies, four games to one.

Ty Cobb was a master at using mind games to gain an advantage over opponents. He was famous for sharpening his spikes before games in plain view of the other team—and then often coming into bases and basemen with those spikes raised high.

TIGERS AT "THE CORNER"

When the Tigers took the field for the first time in franchise history on April 25, 1901, they played in Bennett Park, a small, often crowded stadium situated at the corner of Michigan Avenue and Trumbull Street in Detroit. For almost a full century, the team continued to play at "The Corner" in different incarnations of their original stadium. The first change came in 1912, when team owner Frank Navin invested $300,000 to build a much larger concrete-and-steel stadium on the same site. The new park could hold 23,000 fans—more than double the capacity of Bennett Park. Over the next quarter century,

the stadium (which was named Briggs Stadium in 1938 after new owner Walter Briggs) was modified often, including the addition of lights in 1948. In 1961, with seating now available for 53,000 fans, it was renamed Tiger Stadium, a moniker that stuck for the next 32 years. But on September 27, 1999, the team played its last game on the hallowed corner of Michigan and Trumbull. The Tigers abandoned The Corner for Comerica Park, a $300-million stadium in downtown Detroit designed to combine the classic feel of Tiger Stadium with the newer amenities expected at modern ballparks.

CATCHER · BILL FREEHAN

In 1964, Bill Freehan represented the Tigers in the All-Star Game. He continued to do so for the next 10 years, including 7 as a starter. Freehan, a Detroit native, was most respected for his defensive skills; when he retired, he held the major-league record for putouts as a catcher (9,941) and boasted the highest fielding average for a catcher until 2002. Freehan's bat also matured as he aged. He hit 25 home runs with 84 RBI in 1968, helping lead the Tigers to the World Series. He played a big role in helping the team win the series, too, recording the final out in Game 7 by catching a lazy pop foul.

BILL FREEHAN
CATCHER

DETROIT
TIGERS

STATS

Tigers seasons: 1961, 1963–76

Height: 6-foot-3

Weight: 205

- 11-time All-Star
- 5-time Gold Glove winner
- 200 career HR
- 758 career RBI

TIGERS

FIRST BASEMAN · HANK GREENBERG

Hank Greenberg was never the most graceful player on the diamond. But he made up for his awkwardness in the field with his power at the plate. He hit 40 or more home runs in 4 seasons and walloped a career-best 58 in 1938. Greenberg was one of the first big-league players to join the U.S. Army in 1941 and spent nearly four years serving in World War II.

Despite that absence from the game, he compiled 331 home runs in his Hall of Fame career, then went on to become a general manager and owner of the Cleveland Indians.

HANK GREENBERG
FIRST BASEMAN

DETROIT
TIGERS

STATS

Tigers seasons: 1930, 1933–41,
    1945–46

Height: 6-foot-4

Weight: 215

• 2-time AL MVP

• 5-time All-Star

• 1,276 career RBI

• Baseball Hall of Fame inductee
  (1956)

TWO TIGERS TITLES

obb pursued the AL batting title annually. But in 1921, a new Tigers star, right fielder Harry Heilmann, batted .394 to overtake his teammate for the honor. Two years later, Heilmann topped .400—making him the only Tigers player besides Cobb ever to do so. But even with such strong swingers in the lineup, Detroit spent most of the 1920s stranded near the bottom of the standings.

Twenty-five years after their AL pennant of 1909, the Tigers finally found themselves atop the standings again in 1934—and they did it without slugging outfielder Babe Ruth, whom team owner Frank Navin had desperately wanted to acquire. Instead, he paid $100,000 to sign Mickey Cochrane, who joined the team in 1934 as both catcher and manager. With slugger Hank Greenberg at first and the almost flawless Charlie Gehringer at second, Cochrane led the team to a 101–53 finish, seven games ahead of the New York Yankees. But again, the Tigers were outplayed in the World Series, falling to the St. Louis Cardinals in a defeat capped by a crushing 11–0 loss in Game 7.

Detroit came back with a vengeance in 1935. Greenberg clobbered 36 home runs to win the AL Most Valuable Player (MVP) award and propel the team back to the "Fall Classic," where the Tigers faced the Cubs. Although the Cubs shut them out in Game 1, the Tigers bounced back to win the next three games. The Tigers were determined to not disappoint their fans again—and, finally, they didn't. With Game 6 tied 3–3 in the bottom of the ninth inning, a ringing single by left fielder Leon "Goose" Goslin sent Cochrane hustling home from second base, making the Tigers world champions for the first time.

In 1940, another MVP campaign by Greenberg and a 21-win effort by pitcher Bobo Newsom helped Detroit win the AL pennant by a single game. Then, with the World Series against the Cincinnati Reds tied up at three games apiece, Detroit manager Del Baker asked Newsom to take the mound after only a day's rest. "He called upon his mighty Bobo Newsom, and Bobo, already the dramatic hero of the series, answered the challenge with equal courage," *The New York Times* reported. Newsom pitched valiantly, but Detroit's bats went silent. The Tigers lost the game and series, 2–1.

HANK GREENBERG

Slugger Hank Greenberg was known as the first Jewish star in the major leagues.
He was also known as one of the premier hitters and run-producers of the early
1900s, driving in an incredible 183 runs for the Tigers during the 1937 season.

SECOND BASEMAN · CHARLIE GEHRINGER

Charlie Gehringer's nickname, "The Mechanical Man," was a perfect fit for a player who moved like clockwork at second base and was remarkably consistent at the plate. He was also known as a quiet man who lacked the colorful personality of some of his Detroit teammates. Gehringer preferred to let his talent speak for itself. He led the AL in assists 7 times and fielding percentage 6 times, won the league MVP award in 1937, and hit better than .300 in a season 13 times in his brilliant career. After his playing days, he served as the Tigers' general manager and vice president.

CHARLIE GEHRINGER
SECOND BASEMAN

DETROIT
TIGERS

STATS

Tigers seasons: 1924–42

Height: 5-foot-11

Weight: 180

- .320 career BA

- 1937 AL MVP

- 1929 AL leader in stolen bases (27)

- Baseball Hall of Fame inductee (1949)

As the next season started, so did America's involvement in World War II. The Tigers weren't the only team to lose players to the war effort, but they were hit hard. Greenberg was one of the first players to join the cause, leaving Detroit in 1941. Without their heavy hitter, the Tigers struggled—until a new MVP entered the picture in 1944. Southpaw hurler Hal Newhouser notched 29 wins in his award-winning season, closely followed by teammate Dizzy Trout, who earned 27. Still, the Tigers missed the pennant by one excruciating game.

Newhouser got some much needed help from the offense in 1945 when Greenberg returned in the second half of the season. The team surged ahead of the Washington Senators to win the pennant and take its seventh trip to the World Series. With many players still on active duty in the war, the 1945 World Series was a more low-key event than usual. But with Greenberg back in the lineup and Newhouser on the mound, the Tigers won an exciting series with a dominant 9–3 victory in Game 7. As the last out was recorded, the joyous Tigers rushed the mound to mob Newhouser. For the second time in 11 seasons, the Tigers were the kings of baseball.

BREAKING THE CENTURY MARK

Although the 1934 season ended in heartbreak for the Detroit Tigers, it still ranks as the team's best overall effort. Led by first-year manager and catcher Mickey Cochrane, the Tigers won 21 of their games in April and May. It was in June, however, that the team really began to pick up steam, winning 19 and losing just 8. On June 15, young right-handed pitcher Lynwood "Schoolboy" Rowe earned an 11–4 victory against the Red Sox and proceeded to win his next 15 starts to compile a 16-game winning streak, tying Washington Senators pitcher Walter Johnson's 1912 record. Rowe's streak was complemented by the Tigers' 14-game winning streak in July and August. Along the way, second baseman Charlie Gehringer also compiled the most hits (214) and runs scored (134) in the league. By the time the season ended on the last day of September, Cochrane's Tigers had amassed 101 wins, the most in team history until 1968, when the squad recorded 103. But both the 1968 season and Detroit's 104-win season in 1984 were played on the extended schedule of 162 games, as opposed to the 154 games played in 1934. Therefore, the 1934 Tigers' winning percentage of .656 remains a team record.

Detroit fans would have to wait more than 20 years for another World Series. The Tigers gave fine efforts in 1946 and 1947 but finished second in the AL both years. After the 1946 season, Greenberg moved on to spend his last major-league season with Pittsburgh, leaving Detroit without a bona fide offensive threat.

YOUNG CATS

 year after posting a franchise-worst 50–104 record in 1952, the Tigers signed a promising young right fielder to pull them out of their slump: 18-year-old Al Kaline. Although a slick fielder, the slender youngster struggled at the plate in his first year. Then Red Sox great Ted Williams advised him to strengthen his wrists by squeezing baseballs as hard as he could. The unusual exercise seemed to pay off; in 1955, at the age of 20, Kaline hit .340 and became the youngest player in history to win the AL batting title. "In my book, he's the greatest right-handed batter in the league," Williams said of Kaline. "There's no telling how far the kid could go."

THIRD BASEMAN · GEORGE KELL

George Kell got his big break by being available to play for the Philadelphia Athletics when World War II pulled many big-league players away from their teams. But long after the war ended, Kell remained in the majors, becoming one of the best third basemen of his time. He stole the AL batting title from Red Sox great Ted Williams in 1949, finishing with a .343 average—two ten-thousandths of a point better than Williams. That same year, Kell set a record for the fewest strikeouts (13) by a batting champion in major-league history. He remained with the Tigers as their play-by-play announcer after retiring as a player.

GEORGE KELL
THIRD BASEMAN

DETROIT
TIGERS

STATS

Tigers seasons: 1946–52

Height: 5-foot-9

Weight: 175

- **10-time All-Star**

- **2,054 career hits**

- **.306 career BA**

- **Baseball Hall of Fame inductee (1983)**

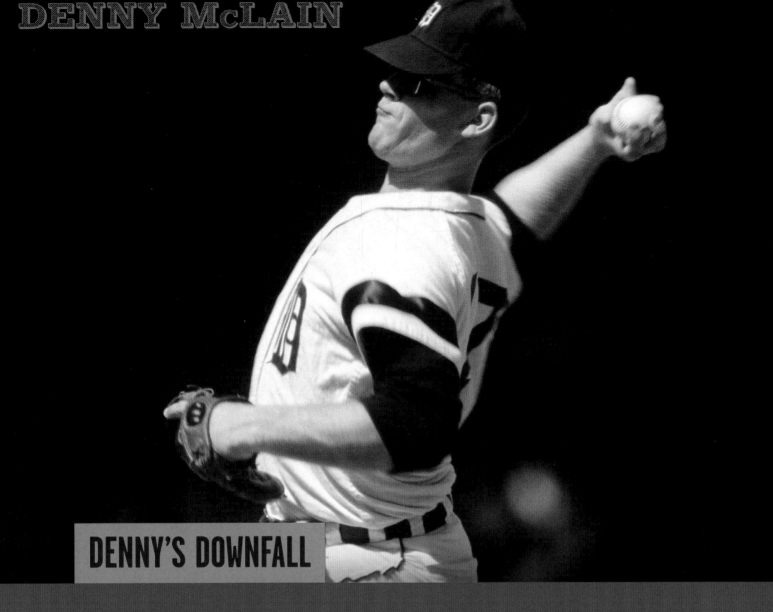

DENNY'S DOWNFALL

Denny McLain had the potential to become the greatest pitcher in Tigers history. The cocky fireballer who wore his hat so low on his forehead that his eyes were barely visible broke into the big leagues with Detroit as a 19-year-old in 1963. By his third season, he was a star, going 16–6 with a 2.61 earned run average (ERA). Three seasons after that, he captured the AL Cy Young Award with 31 victories—a feat no major-leaguer has accomplished since—as the Tigers reached and won the 1968 World Series. The next season, McLain again won the Cy Young Award with a 24–9 mark, but though he was just 25 years old and seemingly entering his prime, he would never have another winning season. McLain, whose hobbies included piloting airplanes, bowling, and playing the organ, also dabbled in disreputable activities such as gambling, bookmaking, and—some alleged—organized crime. He was suspended from baseball in 1970 on 2 separate occasions and was out of the league by the age of 29. Failed business ventures, drug problems, and intermittent jail time followed. "I've got a lot of regret," McLain said from prison in 2002. "I've learned in here that you can't take anything for granted."

Despite the talents of Kaline and infielders George Kell and Harvey Kuenn, the Tigers didn't get higher than fourth place for the next few years. Pitcher Frank Lary led the league with 21 wins in 1956, and Kuenn reigned as the league's leader in hits four times in the 1950s, but the Tigers still struggled to stay above the .500 mark.

In 1961, Tigers first baseman Norm Cash posted 41 homers and 132 RBI to go along with a league-best .361 average, helping his team win 101 games. Unfortunately, that still left Detroit eight games behind slugger Roger Maris and the Yankees in the pennant chase. Thanks to the bats of Kuenn and Kaline, the Tigers put together winning seasons five of the next six years. Still, they truly came close to a pennant only in 1967, when they blew their chance at the AL championship with a loss on the last day of the season.

The Tigers refused to let that late-season heartache haunt them in 1968. After losing on opening day, Detroit went on a 9-game winning streak that set the stage for an incredible 103-win season. Leading the way was brash pitcher Denny McLain; when he won his 30th game on September 14, the crowd at Tiger Stadium stood and chanted, "We want Denny! We want Denny!" until he emerged from the dugout for an ovation. McLain wasn't the only hero, though. Left fielder Willie

Horton led the team with 36 home runs and a .285 average, and the Tigers finished 12 games ahead of the closest AL contender.

Detroit met the defending champion St. Louis Cardinals in the World Series and quickly fell behind, three games to one. But in Game 5, Detroit pitcher Mickey Lolich held the Cardinals to three runs, and Kaline put the Tigers ahead for good with a bases-loaded single in the seventh inning. In Game 6, Detroit scored 10 runs in the third inning and ended up winning 13–1. That set up a tense pitcher's duel in the deciding Game 7: St. Louis's dominant Bob Gibson against Lolich. The game was scoreless until the seventh inning, when a line drive off the bat of Tigers center fielder Jim Northrup cleared the bases. Detroit refused to relinquish its lead, holding on to win the series. Thousands of Tigers fans turned out to welcome the world champions home. "The entire downtown was jammed," McLain later recalled. "There were so many people waiting to meet our plane, they had to close the airport. At the time, the world seemed wonderfully warm."

The warmth didn't last long for McLain. In 1970, he was suspended from baseball for participating in gambling activities and was later sentenced to prison on gambling and drug charges. The Tigers lost another leader when Kaline retired in 1974, shortly after collecting his 3,000th hit. The team struggled, posting a woeful 57–102 record in 1975.

MICKEY LOLICH

BILL FREEHAN

The joyful embrace between pitcher Mickey Lolich and catcher Bill Freehan after the final out of the 1968 World Series became an iconic Tigers image.

SHORTSTOP · ALAN TRAMMELL

Alan Trammell started out as an unremarkable shortstop in 1977. But before long, he became one of the best in the league, pairing with second baseman Lou Whitaker to form the most enduring keystone combination in major-league history: in his 20-year career, Trammell helped turn 1,307 double plays. In 1984, league managers voted him the smartest and best defensive infielder in the game. He helped take Detroit to the World Series that year and, after driving in all four Tigers runs in Game 4, was named series MVP. Trammell returned to the Tigers as manager in 2003 and led the team until 2005.

STATS

Tigers seasons: 1977–96

Height: 6 feet

Weight: 175

- 6-time All-Star

- 4-time Gold Glove winner

- 2,365 career hits

- 1984 World Series MVP

ALAN TRAMMELL
SHORTSTOP

DETROIT
TIGERS

Then, just when Detroit fans needed something to smile about, the Tigers signed a pitcher named Mark Fidrych. Fidrych, who became better known as "The Bird," amused fans and teammates alike with his antics on the mound. He won 19 games in 1976, earning AL Rookie of the Year honors. But it was the conversations that he had with the ball before delivering each pitch that drew fans to Tiger Stadium and attracted media attention. "He was the game's Pied Piper, the most charismatic player I've ever seen in baseball," said Tigers announcer Ernie Harwell. "Everywhere he went that year, people followed in droves. It was phenomenal."

But for all of Fidrych's sweet-talking, the Tigers were able to muster only a 74–87 finish. The next year, Fidrych struggled with injuries, and the Tigers again finished with a losing record. Midway through the 1979 season, the Tigers hired a new manager, Sparky Anderson, who had led the Cincinnati Reds to two world championships. Although Anderson couldn't get his young team above fifth place that year, he began pointing the franchise in the right direction.

LEFT FIELDER · SAM CRAWFORD

Sam Crawford's specialty was the rarest hit in baseball: the triple. In his 19-year career, he tallied 309 three-baggers, still the most in baseball history, just ahead of teammate Ty Cobb. Crawford, a likeable, easygoing player, disliked Cobb intensely—yet the two of them were in agreement when it came to base running, often pulling off daring double steals. Crawford ended his career just shy of 3,000 hits, with 367 stolen bases and 1,525 RBI. He was elected into the Hall of Fame in 1957, thanks in large part to a campaign led by Cobb.

SAM CRAWFORD
LEFT FIELDER

DETROIT TIGERS

STATS

Tigers seasons: 1903–17

Height: 6 feet

Weight: 190

- **2,961 career hits**

- **3-time AL leader in RBI**

- **.309 career BA**

- **Baseball Hall of Fame inductee (1957)**

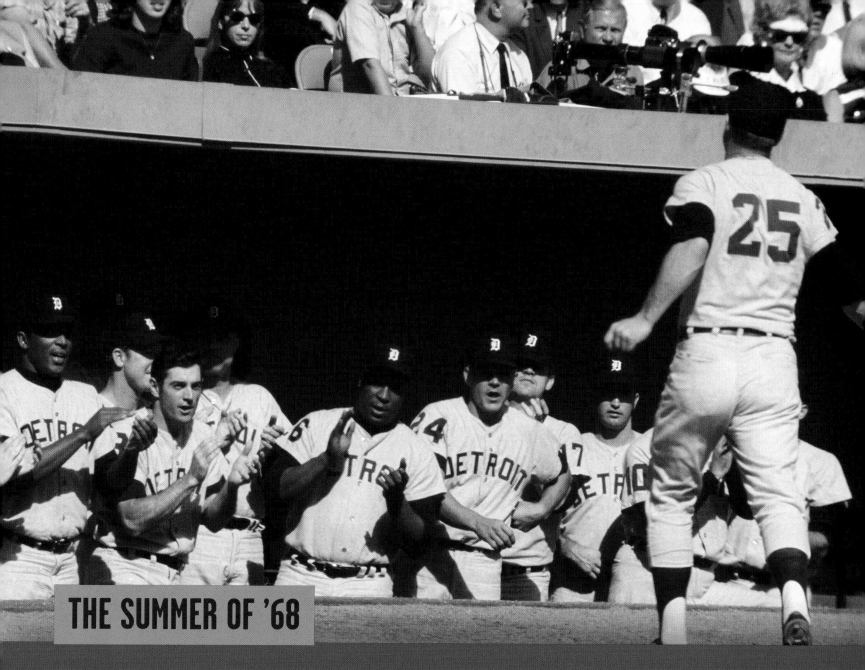

THE SUMMER OF '68

By midsummer of 1968, America needed a pick-me-up. The bloody and controversial conflict in Vietnam was at the forefront of Americans' minds, and the nation was rocked by the assassinations of civil rights leader Martin Luther King Jr. and senator Robert F. Kennedy. Amid so much bad news, major league baseball offered a welcome respite. Sometimes referred to as the "Year of the Pitcher," the 1968 season featured record-setting hurling from the Los Angeles Dodgers' Don Drysdale, who pitched six shutouts in a row; the Cleveland Indians' Luis Tiant, who held opponents to a meager .168

batting average; the St. Louis Cardinals' Bob Gibson, who set a major-league record with a 1.12 ERA; and the Tigers' Denny McLain. That season, McLain went 31–6 with 28 complete games and a 1.96 ERA. In the World Series, Gibson's Cardinals and McLain's Tigers played a magnificent seven-game set in which the Tigers prevailed, beating Gibson in the finale. "I always turn to the sports section first," said Earl Warren, chief justice of the U.S. Supreme Court, in 1968. "The sports page records people's accomplishments. The front page has nothing but man's failures."

GIBSON
23

1984 AND MORE

One of Anderson's first announcements when he took over as the Tigers' manager was that his team would win a pennant within five years—a bold prediction he later admitted he had "pulled out of a bag." But each year, his players progressed toward that goal. Fiery young pitcher Jack Morris began a string of 10 years in which he led the team in wins, including a 20-victory season in 1983. Catcher Lance Parrish and right fielder Kirk Gibson began perfecting their home run swings, while slick-fielding shortstop Alan Trammell and durable second baseman Lou Whitaker became one of the best double-play duos in the majors.

By 1983, the team had broken away from its familiar place in the middle of the pack to finish 92–70, just six games behind the Baltimore Orioles in the AL Eastern Division (the league had been split into two divisions in 1969). And in 1984—exactly five years after Anderson's prediction—the Tigers jumped out to an early lead,

Alan Trammell had few weaknesses as a ballplayer, playing sound defense and winning three Silver Slugger awards as the league's best-hitting shortstop.

buoyed by a Morris no-hitter in the fourth game of the season, and never looked back. By late June, the winner of the AL East was apparent; by the time the season ended, Detroit had compiled 104 wins, eclipsing the Toronto Blue Jays by 15 games.

Detroit swept the Kansas City Royals in the AL Championship Series (ALCS) and then moved on to face the San Diego Padres in the World Series. It took only five games, capped off by Gibson's three-run blast in the eighth inning of Game 5, for the Tigers to claim the world championship. As champagne corks popped in the clubhouse after the game, an emotional Anderson climbed atop a stool to address his players. "Don't forget this moment," he said. "You did it all."

The Tigers would not be able to do it again during Anderson's tenure. They came close during the 1987 season, rebounding from an 11–19 start to capture the AL East crown in the last weekend of play, but they lost in the ALCS to the eventual world champion Minnesota Twins. Detroit remained in the hunt in 1988 as well but couldn't repeat its late-season heroics and finished in second place.

After ending up at the bottom of the heap with 103 losses in 1989, the

CENTER FIELDER · TY COBB

Ty Cobb was one of the greatest players in the history of baseball. He still holds the highest lifetime batting average, a record that is unlikely to be broken, and is second in career hits. He was a daring base stealer who stole second, third, and home in the same inning 4 different times in his 24-year career! Despite his extraordinary talent, Cobb was one of the most universally disliked players in the history of the game. Both teammates and opponents despised him for his hostile temperament and his penchant for hard, spikes-up slides—but they ultimately respected him for his undeniable ability.

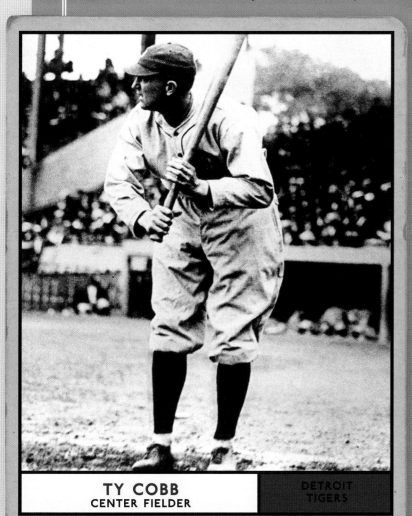

TY COBB
CENTER FIELDER

DETROIT
TIGERS

STATS

Tigers seasons: 1905–26

Height: 6-foot-1

Weight: 175

- .366 career BA

- 4,189 career hits

- 6-time AL leader in stolen bases

- Baseball Hall of Fame inductee (1936)

SPARKY ANDERSON

KIRK GIBSON

PLAYING WITH A SPARK

The Tigers left little doubt that they were a team of destiny in 1984. With skipper Sparky Anderson leading a crew of players cheered on by the popular cry "Bless You Boys" (a phrase coined by local sportscaster Al Ackerman), Detroit made quick work of its opponents, compiling a 35–5 record by the middle of May. Although they had essentially secured the AL East crown by the middle of June, the Tigers continued their winning ways, amassing a franchise-record 104 wins. They quickly added three more to that total by sweeping the Kansas City Royals in the AL Championship Series (ALCS). Then it was off to San Diego to battle the Padres in the World Series. Despite winning Game 2, the Padres didn't have much of a chance; Detroit dominated the rest of the series. Jack Morris pitched all nine innings of both the first and fourth games, holding San Diego to a total of four runs. When the Tigers won Game 5, they notched their 111th win of the season and the 4th world title in team history. The triumph also made Anderson the first manager to win the World Series with both an NL and an AL team.

TIGERS

RIGHT FIELDER · KIRK GIBSON

In the first game of the 1980 season, Kirk Gibson hit both a home run and a triple, setting the stage for what turned into an incredible 17-year career in the big leagues. Although he was never an All-Star or a Gold Glove winner, the scruffy outfielder had a tenacity that made him a favorite with Detroit fans. Gibson had a knack for hitting clutch home runs, including a three-run blast off San Diego Padres pitcher Goose Gossage that sealed a World Series win for the Tigers in 1984. Although Gibson left the Tigers as a free agent in 1987, he returned to Detroit six years later.

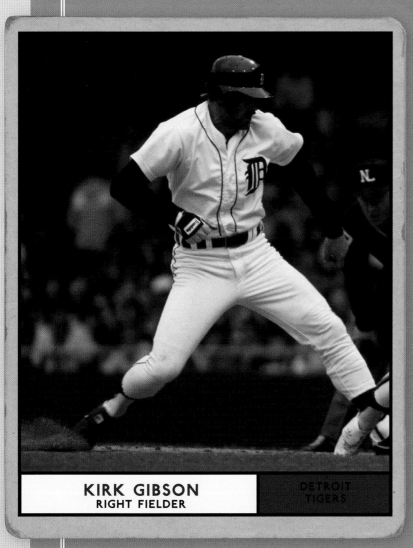

KIRK GIBSON
RIGHT FIELDER

DETROIT TIGERS

STATS

Tigers seasons: 1979–87, 1993–95

Height: 6-foot-3

Weight: 215

- **1984 ALCS MVP**

- **870 career RBI**

- **1,553 career hits**

- **260 career doubles**

Tigers took a risk on big first baseman Cecil Fielder. Fielder's promising career had gone sour in Toronto, but it seemed to sweeten in Detroit. Fielder hit 51 home runs in 1990 and slammed 44 more with 133 RBI as the Tigers finished second in the division in 1991.

The Tigers struggled to contend the next few seasons, and when the 1995 season ended, Anderson announced his retirement. He would be voted into the Baseball Hall of Fame five years later. Anderson's departure was just one of several in the mid-1990s. Gibson and Whitaker both retired in 1995, and Trammell left in 1996. Overseeing a reshaped roster that included hard-hitting outfielder Bobby Higginson and slugging first baseman Tony Clark, manager Buddy Bell began his tenure with a new team record for most losses in a season, as the 1996 Tigers finished 53–109. The slump would continue.

In 1999, the Tigers finished their final season of play in 87-year-old Tiger Stadium before a sold-out crowd of 43,356 fans. The next spring, they opened the 2000 season with every seat filled at their new home, the cavernous Comerica Park. Despite making a competitive showing early in the season, the Tigers faded to finish 79–83.

DETROIT ROARS AGAIN

A fter two more poor seasons, the Tigers hired longtime fan favorite Alan Trammell as manager, but he could not bring back the magic of seasons past in 2003. Instead, the Tigers lost more games than ever before, posting a 43–119 record that set a new mark as the worst in the history of the AL. "We lost a lot of games, but we can't say it was a complete failure," said optimistic rookie pitcher Jeremy Bonderman,

MANAGER · SPARKY ANDERSON

George "Sparky" Anderson played a single season in the majors—in 1959, as a second baseman for the Philadelphia Phillies. But he became better known for his almost 30 years of service as a manager with the Reds and the Tigers. The charming, jovial Anderson led the Tigers to a World Series championship in 1984, won AL Manager of the Year awards in 1984 and 1987, and finished his career in 1995 with the third-most managerial wins in major-league history. Along the way, he earned the nickname "Captain Hook" for his tendency to take pitchers out of a game early and send in relievers.

STATS

Tigers seasons as manager:
   1979–95

Managerial record: 2,194–1,834

World Series championships:
   1975, 1976, 1984

Baseball Hall of Fame inductee
   (2000)

SPARKY ANDERSON
MANAGER

DETROIT
TIGERS

who suffered 19 losses. "A lot of young guys, including myself, have gotten a lot of experience."

The Tigers added to that experience by bringing in such veterans as All-Star catcher Ivan Rodriguez and right fielder Magglio Ordóñez over the next two seasons. In 2006, the rebuilt Tigers were suddenly beasts, going 95–67. A new stable of young pitchers—including Bonderman and fellow starter Justin Verlander—led the charge, along with swift center fielder Curtis Granderson, the team's leadoff hitter. Veterans such as pitcher Kenny Rogers and closer Todd Jones added guidance.

The Tigers clinched a Wild Card berth in the playoffs and then surged all the way to the World Series to face the Cardinals. There, the Tigers split the opening two games of the series before the Cardinals took the next three games to clinch the championship. Tigers fans were disappointed but excited to see what this young lineup could accomplish thereafter. "They're a wonderful group of guys," said veteran manager Jim Leyland, who finished his first season with the Tigers. "We've got a lot of things going right now."

JUSTIN VERLANDER

Verlander thrilled Tigers fans with an early-season no-hitter in 2007 and finished the year 18–6 to cement his reputation as one of the top pitchers in the AL. Ordóñez, meanwhile, won the AL batting title with a .363 average, and Granderson became the first major-leaguer since legendary San Francisco Giants outfielder Willie Mays to record 20 doubles, 20 triples, 20 homers, and 20 stolen bases in a season. But the Tigers' 88–74 record was not enough to bring home another AL Central Division title.

Detroit's record flip-flopped to 74–88 the next season, even though new acquisition Miguel Cabrera, a power-hitting infielder, bashed an AL-best 37 home runs. The 2009 season was a roller-coaster ride for Detroit fans, who saw their team open up a comfortable lead in the division, only to let it slip away to the hard-charging Twins.

With the teams tied for first in the AL Central with identical 86–76 records at season's end, the division was to be settled with a 163rd game, played in Minnesota. The game proved to be, arguably, the most exciting in the major leagues all season. After numerous lead changes, the game went into the 12th inning before the Twins finally plated a

THE FORGETTABLE SEASON

There was good cause for optimism in Detroit at the start of the 2003 season. Alan Trammell, the team's longtime shortstop, had come back to manage the Tigers—and had brought along two of his World Series-winning teammates, Kirk Gibson and Lance Parrish, as coaches. But that optimism quickly turned to despair as the Tigers opened the season by losing nine consecutive games and were saddled with a 3–21 record by the end of April. By the midseason All-Star break, they were carrying a miserable 25–67 mark and had become the laughingstock of major league baseball. Before September even began, the team had already surpassed the 100-loss mark. By the time the schedule mercifully ended, the Tigers were 43–119, setting a new record for the most losses in AL history and coming just one defeat shy of matching the 1962 New York Mets' record of 120 losses. Although 3 Tigers pitchers—Jeremy Bonderman, Nate Cornejo, and Mike Maroth—came close to recording 20 losses, only Maroth actually ended the season with that dismal mark. Fortunately, good news followed bad, as the team rebounded to post a 72–90 record the next year and a playoff-worthy 95–67 mark in 2006.

A native of Venezuela, hard-hitting outfielder Magglio Ordóñez was easily recognized by his long, curly hair until he adopted a shorter cut in 2009.

MAGGLIO ORDÓÑEZ

BRANDON INGE

run to win the game—and the division—by a 6–5 score. Unfortunately, the following season ended sourly for the Tigers as well. Despite the slugging of Cabrera and speed of young center fielder Austin Jackson, injuries led to a mediocre 81–81 mark in 2010.

As one of the true founding franchises of major league baseball, the Detroit Tigers have contributed generously to the game's history. From the days of Ty Cobb to the era of Hank Greenberg to the performances of Justin Verlander, Tigers fans have rarely had to wait long to root for a contender. With a little good fortune and a lot of hard work, today's Tigers just might put Detroit atop the baseball world once again.

JOEL ZUMAYA

INDEX